Your UZZIAH MUST DIE!

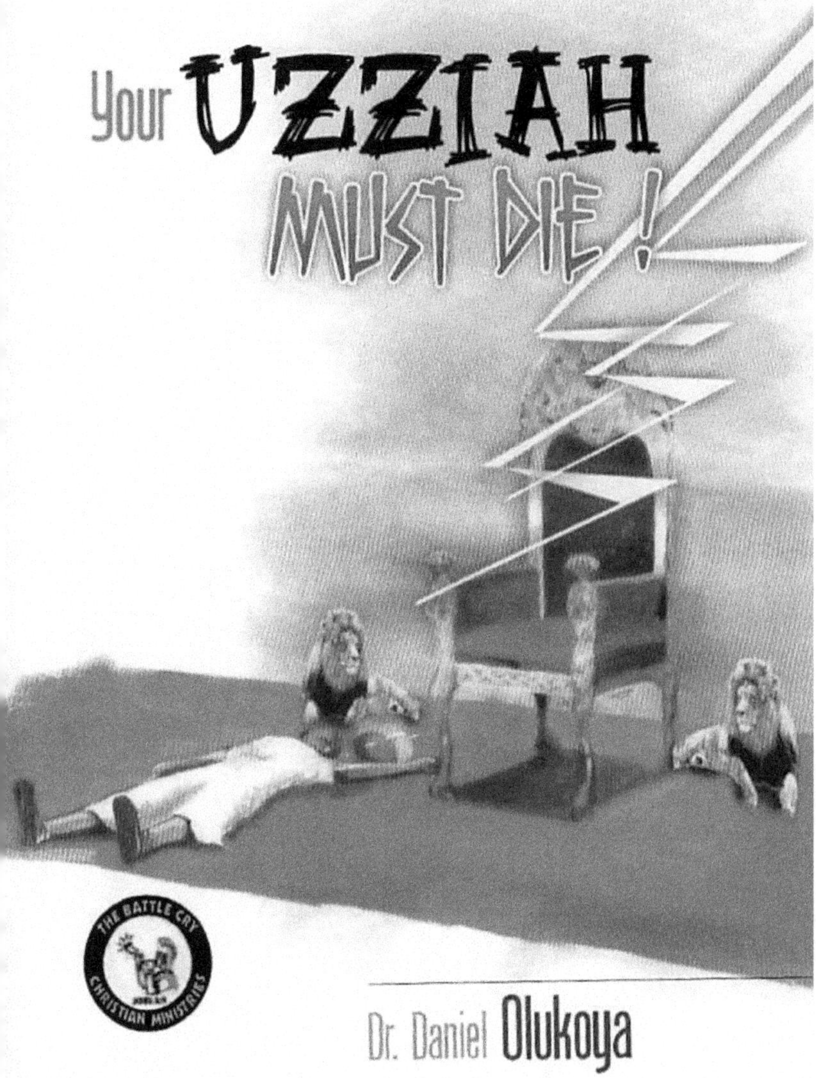

THE BATTLE CRY CHRISTIAN MINISTRIES

Dr. Daniel Olukoya

YOUR UZZIAH MUST DIE!

Dr. D. K. Olukoya

YOUR UZZIAH MUST DIE!

© 2012 DR. D. K. OLUKOYA
ISBN: 978-0692487495
Published - September, 2012

Published by:
The Battle Cry Christian Ministries
322, Herbert Macaulay Street, Sabo, Yaba
P. O. Box 12272, Ikeja, Lagos.
www.battlecrystore.com
email: info@battlecrystore.com
customercare@battlecrystore.com
sales@battlecrystore.com
Phone: 0803-304-4239, 01-8044415

I salute my wonderful wife, Pastor Shade, for her invaluable support in the ministry.
I appreciate her unquantifiable support in the book ministry as the cover designer, art editor and art adviser.

All the Scriptures are from the King James Version

All rights reserved. Reproduction in whole or part without a written permission is prohibited. Printed in Nigeria.

Contents

CHAPTER	PAGE
1. A LIVING SACRIFICE	4
2. THE MYSTERY OF OPEN EYES	15
3. YOUR UZZIAH MUST DIE!	27
4. PARALYSING FORCES	34
5. SPIRITUAL ALERTNESS	43
6. ADULT CRAWLERS	55
7. IMMUNITY SCRIPTURES	66

chapter 1

A LIVING SACRIFICE

Our text is taken from

> Romans 12:1-2:
> *"I beseech you therefore, brethren, by the mercies of God, that ye present your bodies a living sacrifice, holy, acceptable unto God, which is your reasonable service. And be not conformed to this world: but be ye transformed by the renewing of your mind, that ye may prove what is that good, and acceptable, and perfect, will of God."*

A LIVING SACRIFICE

We are all supposed to be what the Bible calls "A living sacrifice." There is a difference between a dead sacrifice and a living one. A sacrifice is something you put on the altar and offer unto God, but a living sacrifice is someone who is on the altar of God. Although the person is still alive, he is dead unto God, that is what we call a living sacrifice. God is saying that there are certain people that he would vomit. You can only vomit what you have not digested. Whenever you eat, your stomach is meant to grind the food into tiny pieces and absorb it. Once that has happened to a particle of food, there is no way it can be vomited again. It has become part of the body.

You can only vomit what your body system has not digested. Vomited people therefore are people who refused to be digested by the Lord Jesus Christ. When you are digested in the intestine of the Lord Jesus Christ, you will automatically be transformed into Jesus. Paul said *(paraphrased)*, ***"I am crucified with Christ, nevertheless yet I am living. But the life I am living now is not me again but Jesus living in me."*** So in order to remain in Jesus, you must leave everything and become like Jesus.

Do you want to remain in the bowel of the Almighty or do you want Him to vomit you? Well, the choice is yours. The Holy Spirit will minister to you through this book, so that anything that makes you or can make you a candidate to be vomited by God will be taken away once and for all-

> Revelation 3:15-16:
> *"I know thy works, that thou art neither cold nor hot: I would thou wert cold or hot. So then because thou art lukewarm, and neither cold nor hot, I will spue thee out of my mouth."*

VAIN WORSHIP

Beloved, the truth of the case is this, the last days are approaching and we must take adequate steps to hinder the progress of the enemies in our lives, by allowing God to digest us thoroughly and completely. I want you to look back at your spiritual life right now. Maybe you have been praising yourself that you are working hard. Unfortunately these days, many preachers are now emphasizing that nothing else should be done apart from praise worship. I have even heard somebody say that the service should be 90% praise worship and the remaining 10% for the collection of offering. They have forgotten that worship from unclean lips is abomination to God. It will even make God angry the more. Praise from adulterous hearts or hearts filled with pride, smell badly in God's nostrils.

They have also forgotten that sinners holding the banners of God with hands filled with sin are nothing other than rebels. You cannot grow spiritually if you just shout and praise. Neither can you experience any spiritual advancement if you do not feed on what the Bible calls "The bread of life."

THE ENEMY'S LADDER

One of the best ladders the enemies use to get into people's lives is found in the Book of John 8:44. It is one of the major reasons why God finds it difficult to digest and swallow some people and thus has to vomit them. It says:

> "Ye are of your father the devil, the lusts of your father ye will do. He was a murderer from the beginning and abode not in the truth because there is no truth in him. When he speaketh a lie he speaketh of his own for he is a liar and the father of it."

> Hebrews 12:1 says;
> "Wherefore seeing we are also compassed about with so great a cloud of witness, let us lay aside every weight and the sin which doth so easily best us and let us run with patience the race that is set before us."

I want you to think about it very well. The verses that we have just read show us that many lives would incur God's trouble and wrath and therefore will not be digested by Him because; somewhere inside those lives are falsehoods of all sorts. No matter how well polished lying and stealing are, they are seen by both God and the devil. A person may ask God to prepare him or her a sanctuary. However, they have not realised that God does not dwell in sanctuaries built with lies.

SPIRITUAL WORSHIP

In the Book of John 4:24, one of the most important verses in the Bible, you can in fact call it the summary of the Bible which says that:

> *"God is a Spirit and they that worship Him must worship Him in spirit and in truth."*

It therefore follows that God can only be reached and worshipped by spiritual and truthful people. Unfortunately, this verse has not succeeded in penetrating the hearts of many Christians, in spite of its deep meaning.

There are so much half-truths and dishonesties in the world today, even among believers in the house of God. Money has made the truth a scarce commodity. The truth you need to know is this; that the purpose of God cannot be carried out in the lives of people who are dishonest. God cannot do anything useful with anyone who practice any form of lying, be it domestic, spiritual, business or diplomatic lies. God will do nothing with such people, rather, He would vomit them.

FAKE BELIEVERS

Many who profess to be Christians are fake believers because they are liars, hypocrites and are grossly deceitful. This sometimes makes one to wonder s, hypocrites and are grossly deceitful. This sometimes makes one to wonder whether or not they are fully converted. Sometimes, even unbelievers will look at some Christians and say: "And you call yourself a Christian, carrying Bible up and down and you are telling lies, useless person." If a fellow human being could say that to you, what do you think God will record in His Book?

It gets me scared and worried that the conversion and the eventual rebirth of so many people have not terminated the nature of sin in their lives. Many truly do not know what they are doing.

When Abraham told lies, little did he know that the act would spread to his son. Isaac also told the same type of lie. He did not know that the repercussion of those lies would be so great. Then his wife Rebecca deceived him too by lying to him that Jacob should be sent away so that he would not marry a heathen woman. The same wife taught Jacob to deceive his father in order to deceitfully receive his elder brother's blessing. Then at an old age, Jacob's sons deceived him as well. When Jacob started his life with deceit, he thought he was being smart.

He stole his brother's birthright by deception. Then the repercussion started; when he went to work, his employer treated him with dishonesty and deceived him into marrying the wrong wife.

LIES AND DECEPTION

Every lie and every deception that you practice will build up trouble for you in the future. Every dishonest notice, thought and action will build up trouble for you.

God can look at a person straight in the eye and know whether there is any falsehood in his or her life. If there is any, He would vomit such a person and once God vomits a person, the person becomes something to be trampled upon by witches, wizards and all kinds of demons.

Remember Judas, he also cast out devils and healed the sick. He was one of those who came back and said to Jesus that the devils were subject to them in His name. Jesus in response said:

> *"Don't rejoice because the devil is subject to you in my name, but rejoice because your names are written in Book of Life."*

So Judas' name was in that Book originally before it was removed. Why? Because he fell out through deceit, lying, theft and hypocrisy.

Remember Balaam, he too was a prophet, but he was covetous and this puts him into trouble.

Remember Samson, he too was used but he got covetous and got killed as a result.

We need to cry out to God asking him to create a new heart within us. In saying this, you must be honest with yourself. God likes honest people.

When Jesus healed the blind man who had been blind since he was born, the Pharisees and the scribes didn't so much like the healing act, particularly as they could not work any miracle. Although, efforts were made to make the blind man to keep quiet, but he did not . He got healed. Their effort was to no avail as the man shouted and confessed and confirmed the healing the more.

The man was honest with himself. A lot of Christians are not honest. They don't pray honest prayers and they don't come to God the way they are. That songwriter said: *"Just as I am, without one plea."* Expose yourself to God today.

chapter 2

The Mystery of Open Eyes

> *I know thy works, that thou art neither cold nor hot: I would thou wert cold or hot. So then because thou art lukewarm, and neither cold nor hot, I will spue thee out of my mouth. Because thou sayest, I am rich, and increased with goods, and have need of nothing; and knowest not that thou art wretched, and miserable, and poor, and blind, and naked: I counsel thee to buy of me gold tried in the fire, that thou mayest be rich; and white raiment, that thou mayest be clothed, and that the shame of thy nakedness do not appear; and anoint thine eyes with eyesalve, that thou mayest see. As many as I love, I rebuke and chasten: be zealous therefore, and repent. Revelation 3:15-19*

Sometime ago, we had a powerful meeting, the kind of meeting which we did along with three days dry fasting. The meeting was for people who desired spiritual gifts. Such meetings were usually started with a prayer point like: "O Lord, give me the spirit of prophecy." On that very day, we prayed so hard that most people who attended that meeting began to prophesy. The Lord opened the eyes of one sister for the first time.

I found that occasionally, the sister would look at the back and quickly turn her face again to the front. Apparently, she was seeing something.

ANGELIC VISITATION

When we ended the service, she came to me and said, "Excuse me sir, immediately we started prayer, one giant man in a white garment was standing at our back with his face shining like fire." I knew immediately that she had seen the angel of the living God. As this same sister was going home, she decided to visit one of her friends who happened to be her prayer partner.

When she got there, her friend served her food which she rejected since she wanted to break her fast at home. She looked into the eyes of her friend and discovered that there was no black pupil inside them. Everything was white. She was very surprised because that was somebody she had been praying with for six years. When God opened her eyes, she then discovered that she had been praying with her enemy.

BLIND EYES

There is no need for you to employ a secretary who is putting blood inside your tea and you are drinking it and thanking God for the tea girl.

> Acts 7: 54-60;
> *"When they heard these things, they were cut to the heart, and they gnashed on him with their teeth. But he being full of the Holy Ghost, looked up steadfastly into heaven and saw the glory of God and Jesus standing on the right hand of God. Then they cried out with a loud voice, and stopped their ears, and ran upon him with one accord. And cast him out of the city, and stoned him; and the witnesses laid down their clothes at a young man's feet, whose name was Saul. And they stoned Stephen, calling upon God, and saying, Lord Jesus, receive my spirit. And he kneeled down, and cried with a loud voice, Lord, lay not this sin to their charge, and when he had said this, he fell asleep."*

They stoned him to death, but their purpose was defeated. Just like on Calvary, instead of destroying the testimony of Jesus, those who crucified Him just magnified it.

Anyone persecuting a Christian is only asking for an explosion. In his death, Stephen cried out like Jesus, ***"Father, forgive them for they know not what they are doing."*** So, Stephen became a corn of wheat that fell into the ground and died. You really have to pray harder now because; men are doing very strange things.

A sister told me that a herbalist asked her to perform a ritual. He told her to put a standard coffin inside a Mercedes Benz V-boot car and drive it right into the sea. I asked her what that action would bring out and she said he said it would bring breakthroughs. I asked her if she did it and she said yes. Wicked men are waxing stronger and stronger and they are becoming very clever in their operations.

EVIL WISDOM

There is evil wisdom in operation all over the place. It is time for deliverance ministers to be able to look straight into a satanic agent's eyes and say, "Oga, that thing that you tried last time, don't try it again. If you do, you will die." The satanic agent will know that an authority is talking and would apologise.

Why is it that many people who desire to encounter Jesus do not see him? Why is it that some people cry out loud and it seems as if Jesus is far away? Let us consider some of the reasons for this:

1. **The state of the stage-** Our mind is like a stage where actors act. Some thoughts are good and some are bad. Sometimes, we cannot prevent certain thoughts from gaining an entry into the stage of our minds, but we have the power to either make them play on or throw them off the stage. So, the first step in committing sin that will block the eyes of a person from seeing Jesus is, indulgence in thoughts that are not pleasing to God. The evil thoughts that do not please the Lord start from the heart. The act of sinning itself starts from the mind. So, once you are committing sin in your thought life, it is as simple as committing it physically. The Bible says that if you lust after a woman in your heart, there is no difference between you and a person who commits immorality physically. The state of our minds may be hidden to others, but they are not hidden to God. We indulge in so many evil thoughts that we ourselves would not want people to know about. It is also on this stage of our mind that battles that will determine our destinies are fought. The powers of darkness like this stage of the mind a lot.

2. **Bitterness and resentment-** If you harbour any of these, it will blind your spiritual eyes and you will not see anything.

3. **Carnality-** Romans 8:6 says, *"For to be carnally minded is death: but to be spiritually minded is life and peace."* If as you read this message you are still going to unbelievers' parties, dancing their dance and celebrating their ceremonies, you are a carnal Christian.

4. **Men pleasers-** There are people who think that they must have the praise and approval of others, regardless of the cost. Yet Jesus said, *"Woe unto you when men say that you are good."* You are invited to where you should not go, but because you are afraid of offending someone you say, "Yes, I will go." Such people spend a lot of time thinking of what people think about them or what people expect from them.

5. **Negative attitude-** A lot of people have negative attitudes towards everything. The world is filled with self-appointed judges and self-appointed referees who criticise others endlessly.

6. **Wearing mask-:** Masks conceal the true identity of people. It is the spirit of pretence, false claim and false profession.

A person who wears a mask becomes a stranger even to himself. It is possible to see somebody holding a pen and a book in his hands in the church, as if he is writing, yet he is sleeping and you will not know. He is wearing a mask. Such a person will say Amen! in the wrong places. A certain man was sleeping as a preacher was preaching. Suddenly, the preacher said anyone that wanted to go to hell fire should stand up, this man who was sleeping, woke up and stood up. He found that he was the only one standing up. Everybody was surprised. He was sleeping when the major part of the sentence was made. He only heard stand up and he stood up. Mask wearers claim to be super spiritual when they are nothing.

The Lord likes people such as the blind man in John chapter nine whom He healed and because he was blind, he did not even know the Man who healed him. When Jesus met him in the temple and asked him saying, *"Believeth you the Son of man?"* He said, *"Who is he Lord, that I may believe him?"* He did not know and he was quite ready to admit. When Jesus' enemies told him that the man who opened his eyes was a sinner, he said, *"I know that God heareth not sinners."* They shouted at him to shut up and asked if he now wanted to teach them the Bible. *"This man did something wrong; why should He heal you on the Sabbath day?"* they said. The man who was healed then said, *"It is wonderful that a sinner could open blind eyes,"* and they threw him out.

7. **Living in the past-** Some people spend the whole of their time living in the past. Such people would say, "If not for that foolish man who made me pregnant in form three, I would not have been here." "If not for the wicked parents who did not send me to school, I would have been a graduate now." How can you allow the mistake that you made twenty-eight years ago to be controlling your life now when you know that Jesus has forgiven you?

The thought of what people would say has produced a lot of spiritual tragedies. For you to please men always, you must wear a mask. I would like to let you know that if you have not pursued your Christianity to a level where someone has called you a fanatic, you have not started. They told Jesus that He was demon possessed, they also told Paul that he was mad.

Therefore beloved, it is time to seek an encounter with the Lord.

> Job 42:5-6 says;
> *"I have heard of thee by the hearing of the ear: but now mine eye seeth thee. Wherefore I abhor myself, and repent in dust and ashes."*

PRAYER POINTS

1. Lord, I want to experience You, in the name of Jesus.

2. O Lord, I want to see You, I want to know You and I want to experience You, in the name of Jesus.

3. Anything hindering me from seeing the Lord, fall down and die! in Jesus' name.

4. I refuse to live in darkness, in the name of Jesus.

5. I reject spiritual blindness and spiritual deafness, in the name of Jesus.

6. Let every spiritual cataract, clear away from my eyes, in the name of Jesus.

7. Father Lord, I want to see You, in the name of Jesus.

chapter 3

YOUR UZZIAH MUST DIE!

"In the year that king Uzziah died I saw also the Lord sitting upon a throne, high and lifted up, and his train filled the temple. Above it stood the seraphims: each one had six wings; with twain he covered his face, and with twain he covered his feet, and with twain he did fly. And one cried unto another, and said, Holy, holy, holy, is the LORD of hosts: the whole earth is full of his glory. And the posts of the door moved at the voice of him that cried, and the house was filled with smoke. Then said I, Woe is me! for I am undone; because I am a man of unclean lips, and I dwell in the midst of a people of unclean lips: for mine eyes have seen the King, the LORD of hosts. Then flew one of the seraphims unto me, having a live coal in his hand, which he had taken with the tongs from off the altar: And he laid it upon my mouth, and said, Lo, this hath touched thy lips; and thine iniquity is taken away, and thy sin purged. Also I heard the voice of the Lord, saying, Whom shall I send, and who will go for us? Then said I, Here am I; send me."
Isaiah 6:1-8

In this chapter, we shall examine what it takes to experience a fresh encounter with God. Note the salient facts in our text.

1.   Have a personal encounter with the Lord: You should be able to say clearly and with certainty, how and when you met God. If you cannot remember when you got born again, it is unlikely that you are. If you are not sure that you are born again, it shows that you are not. Some people say they got born again several times. It is not possible! You are either born again or you are not. A person who gives his or her life to the Lord Jesus, changes. The Bible says, *"he becomes a new creature, old things are passed away and all things become new."*

2.   Your 'king Uzziah' must die!: Anything blocking you from seeing the Lord is a 'king Uzziah'. It is that thing which prevents you from seeing divine revelations. It is the thing that makes you so comfortable that you do not have time to pray or work for God again. It is the thing which occupies your time at the expense of your prayer life and Bible study.

Take this prayer point seriously
- **My 'Uzziah' must die today! in the name of Jesus.**

It does not make sense for anyone who says he or she wants to reign with Christ to be having strange dreams; wherein he or she is having sexual intercourse or is being pursued or is flying. This is not God's plan for His children.

Uzziah stands for pride, over-confidence, etc. Isaiah could not see anything or move forward until king Uzziah died.

3. See yourself as you are: Do not deceive yourself or compare yourself with other people. Peter had fished all night and Jesus came to tell him where to throw his net to catch fish. He did and he caught a lot. It was then that he realised that he was a sinner. He saw himself the way he was. Do not look in someone else' mirror to see yourself. Know who you really are. When you see the real you, you will know who you really are and God will drop His coal of fire upon your tongue, and He will destroy the things that have been limiting His power in your life.

4. Pray for purging: Ask God to purge your life and purify you.

5. Allow the Holy Spirit to possess you: The Bible says: *"Walk in the Spirit and you shall not fulfill the desires of the flesh."* You must lay down all your weapons of rebellion and give full control to the Holy Spirit.

This is a practical message; your tongue is either dead or alive. There is no middle camp; you have either seen the Lord or you have not. You either see yourself the way you are, or you do not see anything.

Right there where you are, ask the Holy Spirit to shine His light upon your life and reveal every hidden sin to you. Every sin of pride, malice, unforgiveness, sleeping with a man or woman to whom you are not married; that is, fornication or adultery, etc. All these are signs of rebellion and until they go, not much can happen.

Uzziah must die! but before that happens, you have to open your life before the Lord. Tell Him who you are; tell Him what you are thinking about, be sincere with yourself so that God can touch you today.

It will be sad beloved, if you take this message lightly and not allow God to touch your life. There is anointing to break every yoke of sin, destroy every bondage of bad habits and remove every cataract from your spiritual eyes, so that you too can say that you have seen the Lord.

When you see the Lord, your life will no longer be the same. For your eyes to see the King of kings, something must happened!

chapter 4

PARALYSING FORCES

There is a department in the demonic world that carries out the function of paralysing people spiritually. These forces are agents. They are listed below:

1. **SATANIC VESSELS:** If God has a duty to perform, He looks for proper vessels to use. Moses was a vessel, Elijah was a vessel and Paul too was a vessel. These three men received spiritual power from on high and transferred them to men. This is why the Bible says, *"How beautiful are the feet of them that preach the gospel of peace."* When a man who preaches the gospel of peace enters a place, his presence ushers in many good things into the place. Likewise, the devil has vessels that he sends to people. He puts dangerous weapons in their bodies to use against the children of God. He sends them to cause confusion in the house of God and even in marriages. Some of the people who come to church are actively working for the devil. For example, gossips, backbiters, liars, etc. They are all working for the devil. I feel sorry for such people because; they can receive what is known as friendly fire. In military terms, friendly fire means an accidental shoot-out against somebody who is in the same camp with you but is looking like an enemy.

There are satanic vessels planted all over the place. They are sent to homes, to break them. A woman brought some materials to us to be burnt. Among the items was a broom which caught my attention. I asked her what it was used for and she said that before she got born again, she was a husband snatcher. When she used the broom to sweep the front of any house she wanted to take over, any woman in charge there would surely leave. These evil vessels are sent to places to cause problems.

It is a pity for a human being to submit him or herself to be used as a vessel by the devil. Vessels of the enemy would cause problem somewhere and when the problem starts, they would be the first sympathizers to arrive the scene. Whereas they were the ones that engineered it. **God will save you from every false friend, in Jesus' name.**

2. **UNFRIENDLY FRIENDS:** A brother thought that he had friends. He was the only one that had a car amongst his friends. He did not know that they were not happy about this. One day, he gave them a lift and dropped them off one after the other at their various destinations. Unknown to him, one of them had put something in the car. As he was passing through a railway crossing and a train was approaching, his car stopped suddenly and refused to move.

He tried to move the car but the car refused to move, so he put the gear in free position, jumped out and tried to push the car away from the track, still the car would not go. Then he called on the God of Elijah and that was what saved him.

Some people's unfriendly friends are sitting on their books, certificates, marriages, promotion letters, academics, careers, etc. As long as they sit on these things, they won't be useful to the owners. Some have friends who would smile at them but in their absence, , they would backbite and disparage them. Such friends are evil vessels and must be dealt with.

There are many people with witchcraft spirit going round looking for people they would harm. One day at a popular bus-stop in Lagos, there was a man selling demonic wares. I watched as he advertised them one after the other. He held up a padlock and said, "With this one, you can lock up anybody. If one person's life does not spoil, another person's life cannot be good. So you must spoil another person's life for yours to become good." He went further to say, "Is it your boss in the office that is annoying you, lock him up so that you can take his position..." I thought nobody would buy, but I was shocked as one man put his hand up and asked how much it costs and he was told N1, 500.00. The man paid for the padlock and took it and asked if there were rules he must observe concerning it. He brought out another one, an animal's horn and after he advertised it, a woman bought it and left. Satanic people selling their wares in a public place!

Some people notice that at certain periods of the night, they feel as if their heads are swelling up and they would not know what is happening- it is simply because there are evil vessels around. Some notice that they are being choked on their beds, while some notice cold feelings all over their bodies. These are signs that there are satanic vessels around and they must be paralysed. Some of these evil vessels transfer demons into people's lives through handshakes. We must avoid such evil handshakes. Those who have no fire in them are most affected by these wicked operations of evil vessels. Make the following declaration before you continue- **"Woe unto that vessel that the enemy will use against me, in the name of Jesus."** So, anyone who releases him or herself as a vessel for the enemy to be used, will have him or herself to blame for whatever happens. Evil vessels convert adults to crawlers.

3. **REMOTE CONTROLLING POWERS-** There are many satanic satellites monitoring the lives of millions. This is why sisters should be very careful about what they put on.

Anything you attach to your hats or dresses that looks like an eye of a fish must be thoroughly checked out. Most of such things are watchers which monitor people. You have to be very careful. A lot of people are being controlled from afar. Those who are directing their lives are not even living in the same town with them. They are far away in dark places doing all kinds of things. If you see the level of satanic wickedness that is going on at night, you would be shocked. Many years ago, my family and I lived in the same environment with a man who had many wives and children. One day, we saw one of his wives with a new born baby and we asked her when she gave birth to the baby, and she said it was the previous day. By the third day, we did not see her with the child again so we asked her about her baby and she said, "Daddy has used it." Used it for what?" we asked her and she said, "For 'juju' (charms)." There are many people like that around. I know something- "My own name is not on the list of candidates for eaters of flesh and drinkers of blood. My name is not on the list of those under demonic control. What about you? There are lots of remote controlling powers operating in our environment. This is why many people fail at the edge of miracles. At the time such people are supposed to move up, the remote controlling powers press a button like that of a television set and they cannot go forward.

Beloved, if you find that as an adult you are crawling instead of walking or running, please pray the following prayer points with holy madness, to release yourself from the grip of satanic vessels.

PRAYER POINTS

1. Every remote controlling power, I dash you into pieces! in the name of Jesus.

2. Every satanic padlock, working against my breakthrough, fall down and perish! in the name of Jesus.

3. Let my prayers provoke angelic violence against my oppressors, in the name of Jesus.

4. I will become all that God wants me to become, in the name of Jesus.

5. Every power hindering my advancement, fall down and die! in the name of Jesus.

6. I move forward in every area of my life, in the name of Jesus.

chapter 5

Spiritual ALERTNESS

Ignorance is no bliss. The enemy will do what he wants to do if you choose to remain ignorant. The Bible says in

> 2 Corinthians 2:11:
> *"Lest Satan should get an advantage of us: for we are not ignorant of his devices."*

SPIRITUAL LAME DUCKS

God wants us to be alert as spiritual soldiers. Victory begins when we have proper estimate of the enemy's capacity. When you go into warfare, you should be able to size up the enemy. When you know the enemy's limit and you fight intelligently, your victory will be swift and decisive.

When a soldier is ignorant concerning the location of the enemy as well as his fire power, such a soldier will experience monumental defeat. My heart goes out to multitudes who attend churches without knowing anything about spiritual warfare. Such people are busy dancing away in ignorance.

The drumbeats of the enemy's war will soon sound against them. The enemy will keep on defeating you until you can come to a point when your hands are taught to do battle.

> Psalm 144:1-2; *"Blessed be the LORD my strength, which teacheth my hands to war, and my fingers to fight: My goodness, and my fortress; my high tower, and my deliverer; my shield, and he in whom I trust; who subdueth my people under me."*

Egypt stands for an unrepentant enemy that has vowed not to rest until he perpetrates his wicked plans. The spirit of Egypt is the spirit of satanic domination. It is the spirit that holds good things under bondage. The spirit of Egypt is the prison house of darkness.

Can you believe that the enemy could be so wicked as to put a whole nation inside a large prison? The Israelites were made up of husbands, wives, family heads, professionals, brilliant young men and women, beautiful and handsome young women and men and promising stars, but the enemy stole their liberty. The least to the greatest were prisoners, they could not spend a day in freedom.

SATAN'S INTENTION

Israel's greatest need was deliverance from bondage. A lot people today are gifted, talented and promising, but such people cannot fulfill their destinies because of bondage.

It is wicked for the enemy to hold a whole nation captive. If not for divine intervention and deliverance of the Almighty, the best men and women in Israel would have spent their entire lives in the jail of the enemy. Israel walked into bondage and coming out was difficult. As far as the devil is concerned, the bondage was supposed to be a life long experience.

COSTLY IGNORANCE

The power of God is incomparable. God, the great deliverer decided to frustrate the token of liars and make evil diviners mad. The totality of the captivity of Egypt was disgraced. There are two problems: we are either guilty of, underestimating the power of the enemy, or guilty of overestimating the power of the enemy. When we underestimate the enemy's power, we behave as if life is a bed of roses and there is no enemy to contend with.

POWERLESS RELIGION

Christianity without warfare can best be described as a powerless religion. How can you say that you are serving the God who is a man of war when the enemy is busy placing your back on the wall and you have no strength to fight back. Even in the Old Testament, David knew that life was a battle, he knew that he had a colourful destiny and he discovered that to fulfil that destiny, he needed to get involved in spiritual warfare.

The secret of victory in life is brought out for emphasis below.

> Psalm 144:2; *"My goodness, and my fortress; my high tower, and my deliverer; my shield, and he in whom I trust; who subdueth my people under me."*

WARFARE SYMBOLS

The Psalmist here gives us a picture of many facets of war. In warfare in Bible days, people needed a fortress, a high tower and a shield. When those things are in place, you are assured of victory. Even in the New Testament, the totality of the spiritual warfare regalia is prescribed for us.

> Ephesians 6:10-17; *"Finally, my brethren, be strong in the Lord, and in the power of his might. Put on the whole armour of God, that ye may be able to stand against the wiles of the devil. For we wrestle not against flesh and blood, but against principalities, against powers, against the rulers of the darkness of this world, against spiritual wickedness in high places. Wherefore take unto you the whole armour of God,*

> *that ye may be able to withstand in the evil day, and having done all, to stand. Stand therefore, having your loins girt about with truth, and having on the breastplate of righteousness; And your feet shod with the preparation of the gospel of peace; Above all, taking the shield of faith, wherewith ye shall be able to quench all the fiery darts of the wicked. And take the helmet of salvation, and the sword of the Spirit, which is the word of God."*

THE COMPLETE ARMOUR

God has given us a complete armour for victory. You need the complete armour to stand against the wicked antics of the enemy. The devil has a well organised army, this is the hierarchy of the enemy's army:

1. Principalities,
2. Powers,
3. Rulers of the dark kingdom,
4. Wicked spirits in high places.

The enemy has given these classes of soldiers the mandate to destroy; it is therefore either the whole armour of God or nothing.

If you want to stand in the evil day, no part of your life must be left unprotected: you need the breastplate, the shoes, the shield, the helmet and the sword. You must learn how to use these weapons in the battle field.

A HIGHER PEDESTAL

Once you are sure you have not underestimated the enemy's power, you must go ahead and solve the next problem. A lot of people are guilty of overestimating the power of the enemy. As a soldier of Christ, there is something you must do before entering the field of battle. You must be conscious of the fact that you have a Commander-in-Chief who has never known defeat. The Bible calls Him the Captain of the Lords host.

The moment you are a member of the Lord's army, you are placed on a higher pedestal; above the army of the kingdom of darkness. You are fighting from a vantage point because before you go into warfare, you are assured of victory. Jesus triumphed over the hosts of darkness, His victory is our victory. Since satan could not overcome the King of kings and the Lord of lords, he cannot overcome you. Going into warfare knowing that the Captain of our salvation leads the fight against the foe will give you uncommon assurance of victory.

SATAN IS DEFEATED

You need this mindset to cut the enemy down to size. Your opponent is weak, he can never be a match for the army of the Lord. Jesus, our Commander-in-Chief has inflicted a fatal blow upon the head of the enemy. Satan is forever defeated. Why then should you behave as if the enemy's fearful credentials are making you shiver?

> The Bible says in Isaiah 31:4-5: *"Now the Egyptians are men, and not God; and their horses flesh, and not spirit. When the LORD shall stretch out his hand, both he that helpeth shall fall, and he that is holpen shall fall down, and they all shall fail together. For thus hath the LORD spoken unto me, Like as the lion and the young lion roaring on his prey, when a multitude of shepherds is called forth against him, he will not be afraid of their voice, nor abase himself for the noise of them: so shall the LORD of hosts come down to fight for mount Zion, and for the hill thereof. As birds flying, so will the LORD of hosts defend Jerusalem; defending also he will deliver it; and passing over he will preserve it."*

THE ENEMY TREMBLES

Egypt is a representative of the army of the enemy. If your enemies are weak, there is no need for fear in your heart. The Egyptians are not unconquerable. Both your enemies and those helping them shall fall. The Bible has likened us to lions; the lion is fearless. The lion cannot be afraid of any animal's voice, hence the Bible had declared that you are only trying to abase yourself by being afraid of elements or powers.

> The Bible says in 1 John 4:4: *"Ye are of God, little children, and have overcome them: because greater is he that is in you, than he that is in the world."*

Although you may be a little child in your eyes, yet you are an overcomer because The Greater One lives in you. In fact, the Bible has declared in

> Romans 8:37 that: *"Nay, in all these things we are more than conquerors through him that loved us."*

UNDER YOUR FEET

The power behind Egypt has been conquered and there is nothing they can do to you. God has positioned you on the side of victory by virtue of the fact that you are a member of the Lord's army. Victory will continue to be your lot. Perhaps you are wondering when this victory will be achieved? The God of war as well as the God of peace shall cause the enemy to be trampled upon and wounded under your feet shortly, in the name of Jesus.

> Romans 16:20; *"And the God of peace shall bruise Satan under your feet shortly. The grace of our Lord Jesus Christ be with you. Amen."*

PRAYER POINTS

1. O God arise! and fight my battle for me, in Jesus' name.
2. I release myself from every generational suicidal tendency, in the name of Jesus.
3. My Father, remove me from the cage of low esteem, in the name of Jesus.
4. I shall not give up, my problem shall give up, in Jesus' name.
5. I bind every evil voice, speaking destruction to my life, in the name of Jesus.
6. Every strongman behind suicide, I bind and pull you down, in the name of Jesus.
7. My Father, deliver me from hearing strange voices, in Jesus' name.
8. Power of sudden death, loose your hold upon my life, in the name of Jesus.
9. Spirit of the living God, arise! and pursue my pursuers, in the name of Jesus.
10. I move from strength to strength, by the power of God, in the name of Jesus.
11. My enemies shall not laugh last over my life, in Jesus' name.

chapter 6

Adult CRAWLERS

As Christians, we cannot afford to sit down and allow the enemy to keep having a field day pulling Christians down, paralysing our prayer lives and throwing away our Bibles in the dream. We must declare to him that enough is enough! Therefore, I would like you to pray these prayer points:

1. I receive the anointing to disgrace every satanic arrow, in the name of Jesus.

2. I refuse to follow the pattern of Samson in my spiritual life, in the name of Jesus.

When your life becomes the electric current of the Almighty, anyone that touches you for an evil purpose shall be electrocuted because it is written: *"Touch not my anointed and do my prophet no harm."* Pray again like this:

- Every strange hand, that has touched my life, wither! in the name of Jesus.

- Every contrary wind, blowing against my life, be silenced permanently! in the name of Jesus.

ADULT CRAWLERS

In these last days, many mighty men are falling. Many that were walking before have been converted to crawlers and those managing to crawl have been completely paralysed. Those who are supposed to be eating bread are drinking milk and those who were drinking milk before are now taking water. These are the last days and the Bible says that there would be perilous times.

The word perilous means difficult to restrain, dangerous, mad, etc. The Bible also says that at this time, evil men shall wax stronger and stronger. They shall be cleverer in their evil designs. The Bible says there shall be intense satanic revival because the devil will put his best possible in his work of destruction.

Beloved, we live in perilous times-

> Habakkuk 1:6-10:
> *"For, lo, I raise up the Chaldeans, that bitter and hasty nation, which shall march through the breadth of the land, to possess the dwelling places that are not theirs. They are terrible and dreadful: their judgment and their dignity shall proceed of themselves. Their horses also are swifter than the leopards, and are more fierce than the evening wolves: and their horsemen shall spread themselves,*

> *and their horsemen shall come from far; they shall fly as the eagle that hasteth to eat. They shall come all for violence: their faces shall sup up as the east wind, and they shall gather the captivity as the sand. And they shall scoff at the kings, and the princes shall be a scorn unto them: they shall deride every stronghold; for they shall heap dust, and take it.*

RETROGRESSION

Our God is a King and kings are fond of raising armies. Here, you can see the kind of army that was raised up by the Lord. It was the kind of army that was not ready to take no for an answer. A part of the passage says, **"...they shall deride every stronghold..."** meaning that they will laugh at the enemy.

Men are supposed to be walking while babies crawl, but now, evil powers have converted many men to adult crawlers and have even made many adults to retire and expire. So, if you must walk and not crawl, you must be violent spiritually. As far as God is concerned, no matter your age, so long you are born again and you are available, He can use you. God is not looking for ability, He is looking for availability. However, if you do not become violent, the enemy can make you to retire and expire.

THE ATTACK

A certain woman was made the principal of one of the best secondary schools in this country. Everything was going on well until one day when a student came to her office and asked her if she was the new principal and she said yes. The girl further asked her whether she was aware of what happened to her predecessor and before she could say a word, she said to her: "Let me warn you. The person who left this place did not pray this sort of prayers you are praying. You know that you do not have fire and you are praying this sort of prayers. You have to be very careful." And before she could stand up to respond, she started feeling dizzy.

The whole office started to turn around before her eyes and she fell on the floor. By the time she opened her eyes, she found herself on a hospital bed with drips. All she could remember was that she was in her office talking to a student. After sometime, she was discharged from the hospital and she went back to school; but right from that day, she started seeing a wall anytime she went out.

The wall would suddenly appear and she would try to push it away and she was the only one seeing it. Even when she wanted to cross the road, the wall would appear and she would stay in the middle of the road trying to push it away, thereby constituting herself a nuisance to other road users.

Her enemies wanted to make her retire and expire before her time.

Make the following confession: **I refuse to expire and the enemy will not retire me, in the name of Jesus.** That was the prayer point the woman prayed and the Lord delivered her. If she had not known what to do, she would be pushing an invisible wall all her life.

A MYSTERIOUS EXPERIENCE

Many years ago, I had the privilege of meeting with a very important person in this country. He came to me crying. I asked what was the matter and he said: "My wife travelled abroad and before she left, she had been warning me about womanizing but I never listened. I wish I had listened to her." What happened? He picked up a girl at a party, took her home and committed immorality with her. As he wanted to go and ease himself in the middle of the night, he discovered that the girl had her two legs on the wall. He tried to remove the legs but they were so heavy that he could not lift them. Then I asked him what he did when he could not lift the legs off the wall. He said: "I broke down and wept because my wife had warned me."

Nobody needed to tell him that he was already in trouble. Eventually, he went for deliverance and God in His mercy, delivered him. He was lucky that he knew the right place to come. He would have expired and would have been retired.

There are so many men who have been retired by powers of darkness. The devil does not respect or know gentleness. Unprofitable gentility must go! You must refuse to make your life a playground for your oppressors. Let me share a testimony with you. Three sisters from the Eastern part of this country noticed that seven people out of the thirteen living in their family died within three months. Only three of them were born again. So they ran to a man of God to find out what was happening.

THE FETISH ATTACK

The man of God prayed and saw a revelation that there was a tree planted in their compound from where they plucked vegetables for food, but a fetish power had been planted underneath the tree. The idea was that anyone who ate its leaves would die. The man of God prayed again to know why the tree was poisonous and the Lord told him that somebody with whom they were fighting over a land did it because he wanted to eliminate everybody so that he would take over the land.

The man of God then asked the Lord what could be done to save the situation. The Lord told them to pray that the fetish thin planted under the tree should be uprooted. The three other people who were not born again went to a herbalist who told them that it was because they did not give a thorough burial to their grandfather that people were dying in the family.

He told them to do a thorough burial and the problem would stop. They were thoroughly deceived.

As they were running around looking for money for the burial, the people of God prayed and the tree dried to the root and the problem stopped and nobody died again. If they were not born again and had gone to do a thorough burial, they would have ended up strengthening their enemy. Pray like this:

1. Every satanic material, buried for my sake, be roasted by fire! in the name of Jesus.

2. Any power carrying sacrifices about against me, be disgraced by the sacrifice! in Jesus' name.

THE POWER OF LIGHT

If you will walk and not crawl, you must become violent. The Bible says that light shines into darkness and darkness cannot comprehend it. Light will always prevail over darkness. Shadows cannot drive light away.

When the sun rises, there is no power of darkness that can go against it. So in a sense, light is more aggressive than darkness.

Christians are meant to be militants and the most aggressive force in the whole of the world. Most often, until you identify what you are fighting and deal with it aggressively, it stares you in the face. Pray this prayer: **I release myself from every demonic ignorance, in the name of Jesus.**

chapter 7

Immunity SCRIPTURES

There is a physical world and there is a spiritual world.

> *"And Jacob went out from Beersheba, and went toward Haran. And he lighted upon a certain place, and tarried there all night, because the sun was set; and he took of the stones of that place, and put them for his pillows, and lay down in that place to sleep. And he dreamed, and behold a ladder set up on the earth, and the top of it reached to heaven: and behold the angels of God ascending and descending on it. And, behold, the LORD stood above it, and said, I am the LORD God of Abraham thy father, and the God of Isaac: the land whereon thou liest, to thee will I give it, and to thy seed;"* Genesis 28:10-13

A man may sleep and another world would open up to him. Sometime ago, we were praying with somebody and a whole human being, wearing rags, walked out of him. We the prayer warriors, including the man saw the thing leaving. It waved at the man and he waved back. Later, and for the first time in his life, he had a financial breakthrough.

It would have been better not to have allowed the spirit to enter him in the first place than for it to enter and he having to go on seven days dry fasting.

More than ever before, we need spiritual and physical immunity. Even in the spiritual world, prevention is better than cure. Some people say that it was because they were living in a particular town that they were having a particular problem; but when they moved to another town, the problem continued. Even when some move to another accommodation, witches would still be pressing them down on their beds. Such people should realise that it is because the enemy has entered inside them. The evil dreams are being played from inside.

IMMUNITY SCRIPTURES

Many believers find it very difficult to memorize the Scriptures. Some will tell you that their brains are getting old, whereas unbelievers spend quality time memorizing incantations which they use against the children of God. The word of God says that, we can build a hedge around us which the enemy cannot penetrate.

There are some passages in the Bible that believers should know offhand, if they want prevention and do not want the enemy to shorten their lives. We call them immunity Scriptures-

Exodus 15:26: says:
"If thou will diligently hearken to the voice of the Lord thy God, and wilt do that which is right in his sight, and will give ear to his commandment, and keep all these statutes, I will put none of these diseases upon thee. Which I have brought upon the Egyptians for I am the Lord that healeth thee."

Deuteronomy 7:15:
"And the Lord will take away from thee all sicknesses, and will put none of the evil disease of Egypt, which thou knoweth, upon thee, but will lay them upon all them that hate thee."

Isaiah 43:2:
"When thou passest through the waters, I will be with thee, and through the rivers, they shall not overflow thee, when thou walkest through the fire, thou shalt not be burned, neither shall the flame kindle upon thee."

This is talking about immunity against the waters of tribulation, immunity against the rivers of trouble and immunity against the fire of affliction.

> Isaiah 54:17:
> "No weapon that is formed against thee shall prosper; and every tongue that shall rise against thee in judgment thou shall condemn. This is the heritage of the servants of the Lord, and their righteousness is of me, saith the Lord."

> Psalm 46:1:
> "God is our refuge and strength, a very present help in trouble."

> Psalm 27:1-2:
> "The Lord is my light and my salvation, whom shall I fear? The Lord is the strength of my life; of whom shall I be afraid?. When the wicked, even mine enemies and my foes came upon me to eat up my flesh, they stumbled and fell."

> Psalm 91:1:
> *"He that dwelleth in the secret place of the most high shall abide under the shadow of the Almighty."*

Psalm 91 tells us about immunity against the power of the night. It might interest you to know that most people do not sleep at night. The Psalms also talk about the arrow that flies by the day. It tells us about immunity against pestilence that walks about in darkness. It tells us about the power that causes destruction at noonday. It talks about power against the serpent and the dragon. It talks about immunity against evil in all its ramification.

> Psalm 105: 14-15:
> *"He suffered no man to do them wrong, yea he reproved kings for their sake, saying, Touch not my anointed and do my prophet no harm."*

> Zechariah 2:5:
> *"For I saith the Lord will be unto her a wall of fire around about her and will be the glory in the midst of her."* Verse

8: *"For thus saith the Lord of hosts, after the glory hath he sent me unto the nations, which soiled you for he that toucheth you toucheth the apple of his eyes."*

Psalm 34:7:
"The angel of the Lord encampeth around about them that fear him and delivereth them."

Proverbs 3:24:
"When thou liest down, thou shalt not be afraid; yea, thou shalt lie down, and thy sleep shall be sweet."

Mark 16:18:
"They shall take up serpents and if they drink any deadly thing it shall not hurt them, they shall lay hands on the sick, and they shall recover."

Luke 10:19:
"Behold I give unto you power to tread upon serpents and scorpions and over all the power of the enemy and nothing shall by any means hurt you."

SPIRITUAL IMMUNITY

My prayer is that your spiritual immunity shall not break down, in Jesus' name. We have so many outstanding promises that God will protect us, but if we break certain laws, this immunity will break down. If you don't know what to do or you do the wrong thing, your immunity can break down. So many things can break down the immunity. For example, wrong attitude. If somebody hurts you and you harbour resentment in your heart against him/her, the enemy can see the dark cloud in your heart and that will break down your immunity.

Following the fashion of the world is another way you can break down your immunity. When someone lets you down or disappoints you and you begin to broadcast it to the whole world, your immunity will break down. When you pay evil for evil; when you decide to pay people back in their own coin, your immunity will break down.

WHEN IMMUNITY BREAKS DOWN

When you are very angry and you throw temper tantrum, your immunity will break down. Calling people insulting names, gossiping and not forgiving those that have hurt you will make your immunity to break down. All the demonic jewelry that people put on makes their immunity to break down. Demonic herbal concoctions and other terrible things that people swallow make their immunity to break down.

> Leviticus 17:11:
> *"For the life of the flesh is in the blood and I have given it to you upon the altar to make an atonement for your souls, for it is the blood that maketh an atonement for the soul."*

For you to be healthy and be moving about without any sickness, your blood must be immuned. All the diseases that are available actually drink people's blood. If a person loses a lot of blood and nothing is done to restore it, he will soon die. Malaria is a terrible disease because it sucks people's blood and uses it to produce more of its kind. Surely every sickness came as a result of the failure of Adam and Eve.

Somebody had a fever in the Bible. Let us see what Jesus did-

> Luke 4:38:
> *"And he arose out of the synagogue, and entered into Simon's house. And Simon's wife's mother was taken with a great fever and they besought him for her. And he stood over her and rebuked the fever and it left her and immediately she arose and ministered unto them."*

It means that you can talk to the fever or to your blood. You may say that this is madness. That would not be strange, after all, people said that Jesus and Paul were mad. When you learn to pray the following prayer points, you give yourself immunity:

1. Let the blood of Jesus be transfused into my blood, in Jesus' name.

2. I render my blood untouchable to any disease, in Jesus' name.

When you pray in this manner, any disease that comes in contact with your blood will die. There are so many other things that you can do. For example, you can anoint your body or put the anointing oil in your cream. You must be careful about the kind of food you eat. You must always pray on your food and your water and make sure you don't overeat.

The children of darkness often fortify and prepare themselves because they know that they can be attacked, but sometimes, the children of God are so foolish that they don't fortify themselves. In the light of this, I want you to pray the following prayer points aggressively.

PRAYER POINTS

1. *(Lay your hands on your head):* I challenge my body with the fire of God, in Jesus' name.

2. Every evil eternal enemy, come out by fire! in the name of Jesus.

3. O God, establish your kingdom in every department of my life, in the name of Jesus.

Other Publication By Dr. D. K. Olukoya

1. 20 Marching Orders To Fulfill Your Destiny
2. 30 Prophetic Arrows From Heaven
3. 30 Things The Anointing Can Do For You
4. Abraham's Children in Bondage
5. A-Z of Complete Deliverance
6. Basic Prayer Patterns
7. Be Prepared
8. Bewitchment must Die
9. Biblical Principles of Dream Interpretation
10. Born Great, But Tied Down
11. Breaking Bad Habits
12. Breakthrough Prayers For Business Professionals
13. Bringing Down The Power of God
14. Brokenness
15. Can God Trust You?
16. Command The Morning
17. Connecting to The God of Breakthroughs
18. Consecration Commitment & Loyalty
19. Contending For The Kingdom
20. Criminals In The House Of God
21. Dancers At The Gate of Death
22. Dealing Destiny Vultures
23. Dealing With Destiny Thieves
24. Dealing With Hidden Curses
25. Dealing With Local Satanic Technology
26. Dealing With Satanic Exchange
27. Dealing With The Evil Powers Of Your Father's House
28. Dealing With Tropical Demons
29. Dealing With Unprofitable Roots
30. Dealing With Witchcraft Barbers

Other Publication By Dr. D. K. Olukoya

31. Deep Secrets, Deep Deliverance
32. Deliverance By Fire
33. Deliverance From Evil Foundation
34. Deliverance From Spirit Husband And Spirit Wife
35. Deliverance From The Limiting Powers
36. Deliverance of The Brain
37. Deliverance Of The Conscience
38. Deliverance Of The Head
39. Deliverance of The Tongue
40. Deliverance: God's Medicine Bottle
41. Destiny Clinic
42. Destroying Satanic Masks
43. Disgracing Soul Hunters
44. Divine Military Training
45. Divine Prescription For Your Total Immunity
46. Divine Yellow Card
47. Dominion Prosperity
48. Drawers Of Power From The Heavenlies
49. Evil Appetite
50. Evil Umbrella
51. Facing Both Ways
52. Failure In The School Of Prayer
53. Fire For Life's Journey
54. For We Wrestle ...
55. Freedom Indeed
56. God's Key To A Happy Life
57. Healing Through Prayers
58. Holiness Unto The Lord
59. Holy Cry
60. Holy Fever

OTHER PUBLICATION BY DR. D. K. OLUKOYA

61. Hour Of Decision
62. How To Obtain Personal Deliverance
63. How To Pray When Surrounded By The Enemies
64. I Am Moving Forward
65. Idols Of The Heart
66. Igniting Your Inner Fire
67. Is This What They Died For?
68. Kill Your Goliath By Fire
69. Killing The Serpent of Frustration
70. Let Fire Fall
71. Let God Answer By Fire
72. Limiting God
73. Lord, Behold Their Threatening
74. Madness of The Heart
75. Making Your Way Through The Traffic Jam of Life
76. Meat For Champions
77. Medicine For Winners
78. My Burden For The Church
79. Open Heavens Through Holy Disturbance
80. Overpowering Witchcraft
81. Paralysing The Riders And The Horse
82. Personal Spiritual Check-Up
83. Possessing The Tongue of Fire
84. Power Against Coffin Spirits
85. Power Against Destiny Quenchers
86. Power Against Dream Criminals
87. Power Against Local Wickedness
88. Power Against Marine Spirits
89. Power Against Spiritual Terrorists
90. Power Against The Mystery of Wickedness

91. Power Against Unclean Spirits
92. Power Must Change Hands
93. Power of Brokenness
94. Power To Disgrace The Oppressors
95. Power To Recover Your Birthright
96. Power To Recover Your Lost Glory
97. Power To Shut Satanic Doors
98. Pray Your Way To Breakthroughs
99. Prayer Strategies For Singles
100. Prayer Is The Battle
101. Prayer Rain
102. Prayer To Kill Enchantment
103. Prayer To Make You Fulfill Your Divine Destiny
104. Prayer Warfare Against 70 Mad Spirits
105. Prayers For Open Heavens
106. Prayers To Destroy Diseases And Infirmities
107. Prayers To Move From Minimum To Maximum
108. Praying Against Foundational Poverty
109. Praying Against The Spirit Of The Valley
110. Praying In The Storm
111. Praying To Destroy Satanic Roadblocks
112. Praying To Dismantle Witchcraft
113. Principles of Conclusive Prayers
114. Principles Of Prayer
115. Raiding The House of The Strongman
116. Release From Destructive Covenants
117. Revoking Evil Decrees
118. Safeguarding Your Home
119. Satanic Diversion Of The Black Race
120. Secrets of Spiritual Growth And Maturity

121. Setting The Covens Ablaze
122. Seventy Rules of Spiritual Warfare
123. Seventy Sermons To Preach To Your Destiny
124. Silencing The Birds Of Darkness
125. Slave Masters
126. Slaves Who Love Their Chains
127. Smite The Enemy And He Will Flee
128. Speaking Destruction Unto The Dark Rivers
129. Spiritual Education
130. Spiritual Growth And Maturity
131. Spiritual Warfare And The Home
132. Stop Them Before They Stop You
133. Strategic Praying
134. Strategy Of Warfare Praying
135. Students In The School Of Fear
136. Symptoms Of Witchcraft Attack
137. Taking The Battle To The Enemy's Gate
138. The Amazing Power of Faith
139. The Baptism of Fire
140. The Battle Against The Spirit Of Impossibility
141. The Chain Breaker
142. The Dinning Table Of Darkness
143. The Enemy Has Done This
144. The Evil Cry Of Your Family Idol
145. The Fire Of Revival
146. The Gateway To Spiritual Power
147. The Great Deliverance
148. The Hidden Viper
149. The Internal Stumbling Block
150. The Lord is A Man of War

151. The Mystery Of Mobile Curses
152. The Mystery Of The Mobile Temple
153. The Power of Aggressive Prayer Warriors
154. The Power of Priority
155. The Prayer Eagle
156. The Pursuit Of Success
157. The Scale of The Almighty
158. The School of Tribulation
159. The Seasons Of Life
160. The Secrets Of Greatness
161. The Serpentine Enemies
162. The Skeleton In Your Grandfather's Cupboard
163. The Slow Learners
164. The Snake In The Power House
165. The Spirit Of The Crab
166. The Star Hunters
167. The Star In Your Sky
168. The Terrible Agenda
169. The Tongue Trap
170. The Unconquerable Power
171. The University of Champions
172. The Unlimited God
173. The Vagabond Spirit
174. The Way Of Divine Encounter
175. The Wealth Transfer Agenda
176. Tied Down In The Spirits
177. Too Hot To Handle
178. Turnaround Breakthrough
179. Unprofitable Foundations
180. Victory Over Satanic Dreams

OTHER PUBLICATION BY DR. D. K. OLUKOYA

181. Victory Over Your Greatest Enemies
182. Violent Prayers Against Stubborn Situations
183. War At The Edge Of Breakthroughs
184. Wasted At The Market Square of Life
185. Wasting The Wasters
186. Wealth Must Change Hands
187. What You Must Know About The House Fellowship
188. When God Is Silent
189. When The Battle is from Home
190. When The Deliverer Need Deliverance
191. When The Enemy Hides
192. When Things Get Hard
193. When You Are Knocked Down
194. When You Are Under Attack
195. When You Need A Change
196. Where Is Your Faith?
197. While Men Slept
198. Woman! Thou Art Loosed.
199. Your Battle And Your Strategy
200. Your Foundation And Destiny
201. Your Mouth And Your Deliverance
202. Your Mouth And Your Warfare

YORUBA PUBLICATIONS

1. Adura Agbayori
2. Adura Ti Nsi Oke Ni' di
3. Ojo Adura

OTHER PUBLICATION BY DR. D. K. OLUKOYA

FRENCH PUBLICATIONS

1. Bilan Spirituel Personnel
2. Cantique Des Contiques
3. Commander Le Matin
4. Comment Recevior La Delivrance Du Mari Et Femme De Nuit
5. Cpmment Se Delivrer Soi-meme
6. Demanteler La Sorcellerie
7. En Finir Avec Les Forces Malefiques De La Maison De Ton Pere
8. Espirit De Vagabondage
9. Femme Tu Es Liberee
10. Frappez l'adversaire Et Il Fuira
11. L'etoile Dans Votre Ciel
12. La Deliverance De La Tete
13. La Deliverance: Le Flacon De Medicament Dieu
14. La Deviation Satanique De La Race Noire
15. Le Combat Spirituel Et Le Foyer
16. Le Mauvais Cri Des Idoles
17. Le Programme De Tranfert De Richesse
18. Les Etudiants A l'ecole De La Peur
19. Les Saisons De La Vie
20. Les Strategies De Prieres Pour Les Celibataires
21. Ne Grand Mais Lie
22. Pluie De Priere
23. Pouvoir Contre Les Demond Tropicaux
24. Povoir Contre Les Terrorites Spirituel
25. Prier Jusqu'a Remporter La Victoire
26. Priere De Percees Pour Les Hommes D'affaires
27. Priere Pour Detruire Les Maladies Et Infirmites
28. Prieres Violentes Pour Humilier Les Problemes Opiniatres

OTHER PUBLICATION BY DR. D. K. OLUKOYA

29. Prieres De Comat Contre 70 Espirits Dechanines
30. Quand Les Choses Deviennent Difficiles
31. Que l'envoutement Perisse
32. Revoquer Les Decrets Malefiques
33. Se Liberer Des Alliances Malefiques
34. Ton Combat Et Ta Strategie
35. Victoires Sur Les Reves Sataniques
36. Votre Fondement Et Votre Destin

ANNUAL 70 DAYS PRAYER AND FASTING PUBLICATIONS

1. Prayers That Bring Miracles
2. Let God Answer By Fire
3. Prayers To Mount With Wings As Eagles
4. Prayers That Bring Explosive Increase
5. Prayers For Open Heavens
6. Prayers To Make You Fulfill Your Divine Destiny
7. Prayers That Make God To Answer And Fight By Fire
8. Prayers That Bring Unchallengeable Victory And Breakthrough Rainfall Bombardments
9. Prayers That Bring Dominion Prosperity And Uncommon Success
10. Prayers That Bring Power And Overflowing Progress
11. Prayers That Bring Laughter And Enlargement Breakthroughs
12. Prayers That Bring Uncommon Favour And Breakthroughs
13. Prayers That Bring Unprecedented Greatness And Unmatchable Increase
14. Prayers That Bring Awesome Testimonies And Turn Around Breakthroughs
15. Prayers That Bring Glorious Restoration
16. Prayers That Bring Unrivaled Lifting

PUBLICATIONS BY PASTOR (MRS.) SHADE OLUKOYA

1. Daughters of Philip
2. I Decree An Uncommon Change
3. Power To Fulfil Your Destiny
4. Principles of A Successful Marriage
5. The Call of God
6. When Your Destiny Is Under Attack
7. Woman of Wonder
8. Violence Against Negative Voices

The Books, Tapes and CDs (Audio and Video) All Obtainable At:

☞ **Battle Cry Christian Ministries**
322, Herbert Macaulay Way, Sabo, Yaba, Lagos
Phone: 01 8044415, 0803 304 4239

☞ **MFM International Bookshop**
13, Olasimbo Street, Onike, Yaba, Lagos

☞ **MFM Prayer City**
Km 12, Lagos/Ibadan Expressway

☞ **54, Akeju Street, off Shipeolu Street**
Palmgrove, Lagos

☞ **All MFM Churches Nationwide**

☞ **All Leading Christian Bookstores**

BOOK ORDER

*Is there any book written by
Dr. D. K. Olukoya (General Overseer, MFM Ministries)
that you would like to have:*

Have you seen his latest books?

To place an order for this End-Time Materials,

Call: 08161229775

Battle Cry Ministries... equipping the saints of God

God bless.

www.ingramcontent.com/pod-product-compliance
Lightning Source LLC
LaVergne TN
LVHW051156080426
835508LV00021B/2665